TABLE OF CONTENTS

There are no names on the cover of this book because it would not be possible to fit the names of everyone who helped make it happen. This book came about thanks to the adventurous parents, colleagues, and friends of young math who took our original classes, play-tested our ideas, asked deep questions, crowdfunded the making of the book, guest blogged on our site, shared their concerns, and sent us their and their kids' thoughts about the games.

Anonymous
Aaron Silvers
Adam Hansen
Alexander Bogomolny
Alexander Rozenfeld
Algot Runeman
Ali Rosselle
Allison Krasnow
Andrius Kulikauskas
Angela Stauder
Ann Lettes
Anna Weltman
Anne Jeanette Martin
Arkadiy Birger
Axelle Faughn
Barbara Schindelhauer
Bettina Bowers Schwan
Bonnie Crowder
Boris Brodsky
Brad Morgan
Brandy Wiegers
Brenda Weiss
Brian Turley
Colin Chambers
Carles Aguilo Collado
Carol Cross
Chris Hunter
Christian McManaman
Christine Cobb
Colleen King
Dani Novak
Daniel Patterson
David Cordeiro
David Wees
Deborah Cohen
Denise Gaskins
Dmitri Droujkov

Dmitri Kazmin
Dmitry Sagalovskiy
Dor Abrahamson
Elena Bazarova
Elena Koldertsova
Elisa Wing
Elizabeth Ross
Elizabeth Zwicky
Ever Salazar
Fred Bishop
George Vennebush
Gina Goddard
Gordon Hutchinson
Heather Chapman
Heidi Van Natter
Hope McMullan
Hope Thompson
Irina Mokrova
James Laidlaw
Jason Holder
Jenny Eggleston
Joel Duffin
John Domar
John Golden
Julia Brodsky
Joshua Zucker
Kelli Brandon
Kelly Prak
Kialei
Kimberley Meltzer
Kimberly Naylor
Laura Overdeck
Lee Ann Dietz
Lucy Laffitte
Madison Cross Sugg
Malke Rosenfeld
Maria Linnik

Maria Muscarella
Marie Brodsky
Marjalee Smith
Mary Malpezzi
Matt Droujkov
Max Leisten
Melanie Hayes
Michael Rachkovsky
Michael Thayer
Mike Graham
Nancy Ruhana
Nicole Smith
Noelle Cahow
Nora Reynolds
Patrick Honner
Paul Solomon
Pete Longhurst
Porter Family
Richard Elwes
Royce Riddle
Ryan Combs
Sara Joy Pond
Sara McGrath
Science Jim
Sharon Vogt
Sheri Soffian
Sol Lederman
Stacy Perry
Stephen Thomas
Sue Stern
Sue Van Hattum
Suellen DiMassimo
Susan Mygatt
Terri Coons
Vitomir Stojanovski
Zhuo Hong

WHY PLAY THIS BOOK

Children dream big. They crave exciting and beautiful adventures to pretend-play. Just ask them who they want to be when they grow up. The answers will run a gamut from astronauts to zoologists and from ballerinas to Jedi masters. So how come children don't dream of becoming mathematicians?

Kids don't dream of becoming mathematicians because they already are mathematicians. Children have more imagination than it takes to do differential calculus. They are frequently all too literate like logicians and precise like set theorists. They are persistent, fascinated with strange outcomes, and are out to explore the "what-if" scenarios. These are the qualities of good mathematicians!

As for mathematics itself, it's one of the most adventurous endeavors a young child can experience. Mathematics is exotic, even bizarre. It is surprising and unpredictable. And it can be more exciting, scary, and dangerous than sailing on high seas!

But most of the time math is not presented this way. Instead, children are required to develop their mathematical skills rather than being encouraged to work on something more nebulous, like the mathematical state of mind. Along the way the struggle and danger are de-emphasized, not celebrated – with good intentions, such as safety and security. In order to achieve this, children are introduced to the tame, accessible scraps of math, starting with counting, shapes, and simple patterns. In the process, everything else mathematical gets left behind "for when the kids are ready." For the vast majority of kids, that readiness never comes. Their math stays simplified, impoverished, and limited. That's because you can't get there from here. If you don't start walking the path of those exotic and dangerous math adventures, you never arrive.

It is as tragic as if parents were to read nothing but the alphabet to children, until they are "ready" for something more complex. Or if kids had to learn "The Itsy-Bitsy Spider" by heart before being allowed to listen to any more involved music. Or if they were not allowed on any slide until, well, learning to slide down in completely safe manner. This would be sad and frustrating, wouldn't it? Yet that's exactly what happens with early math. Instead of math adventures – observations, meaningful play, and discovery of complex systems – children get primitive, simplistic math. This is boring not only to children, but to adults as well. And boredom leads to frustration. The excitement of an adventure is replaced by the gnawing anxiety of busy work.

We want to create rich, multi-sensory, deeply mathematical experiences for young children. The activities in this book will help you see that with a bit of know-how every parent and teacher can stage exciting, meaningful and beautiful early math experiences. It takes no fancy equipment or software beyond everyday household or outdoor items, and a bit of imagination – which can be borrowed from other parents in our online community. You will learn how to make rich mathematical properties of everyday objects accessible to young children. Everything around you becomes a learning tool, a prompt full of possibilities for math improvisation, a conversation starter. The everyday world of children turns into a mathematical playground.

Children marvel as snowflakes magically become fractals, inviting explorations of infinity, symmetry, and recursion. Cookies offer gameplay in combinatorics and calculus. Paint chips come in beautiful gradients, and floor tiles form tessellations. Bedtime routines turn into children's first algorithms. Cooking, then mashing potatoes (and not the other way around!) humorously introduces commutative property. Noticing and exploring math becomes a lot more interesting, even addictive. Unlike simplistic math that quickly becomes boring, these deep experiences remain fresh, because they grow together with children's and parents' understanding of mathematics.

Can math be interesting? A lot of it already is! Can your children be strong at advanced math? They are natural geniuses at some aspects of it! Your mission, should you accept it: to join thrilling young math adventures! Ready? Then let's play!

QUESTIONS & ANSWERS

How can I help my child to solve math problems?

Use modeling, especially with young kids. Represent the problem with objects and toys, or roleplay it with people. Use drawings and paper models, too. Different colors can stand for different mathematical features of the problem. Retell the problem as a story with characters, if your child likes fiction. Make simple diagrams out of objects by lining up toys or using sorting grids, and use pictures to make timelines (such as bedtime routine). Capture math processes, such as sorting, as series of photos.

What should I do when my child makes a mistake?

Any story, number, shape is an example of some math. It may not be the example you were originally looking for, but that's OK. Take the answer and love it and find a problem that would fit it. Another good exercise: for a month or two, don't ask questions for which you know answers. If you really feel the urge to ask "What is two plus three?" rephrase as, "What would you make two plus three be, and why?" Investigate all answers. You will learn a lot about math and about your kid!

When I ask my child a word problem she always solves it, but if I pose the same problem as an equation, say 2+3=?, she doesn't know what to do. Why?

Because you broke The Rule of Three! Any idea needs at least three very different examples, more for young kids. In this case, you offered two examples of seeing the problem: stories and numbers. Offer more examples, and make them varied! Try jumps (two jumps and three jumps), lengths (two units and three units), counters (two raisins and three raisins), sounds (two claps and three claps), and so on.

3

How can I make math engaging? How do I help my kid love math?

<u>Find math you love</u>. There is some out there, for sure. Try artistic math videos, puzzles, apps, and games. Use math to make money, to hack your computer, to bring social justice to your city – any cause you find worthwhile, or at least cool. After you figure out how to be a good math role model, find math in activities your kid already likes, as well.

How do you collect math manipulatives without feeling overwhelmed by "stuff"?

<u>Reuse and recycle!</u> Many regular household items make excellent math manipulatives and game props. For example, cups and spoons provide gradients; stairs can become a number line. <u>Dedicate a box or a basket</u> to math treasures (such as shells of different colors and shapes) and math tools (such as a ruler, a compass, and graph paper). This way, the kid can grab the manipulatives and start working right away.

Does teaching a young child to count or to instantly recognize a group of dots undermine deeper mathematical learning?

<u>Here are the four main ways toward building the basic concept of number:</u>
- <u>subitizing</u> – the ability to instantly recognize quantities without counting
- <u>counting</u> – addition and subtraction are all about sequences: dealing with objects one-by-one
- <u>unitizing</u> – multiplication and division are based on equal groups or units
- <u>exponentiating</u> – self-similar structures, such as fractals

None of these ways toward number is dangerous in itself. The lack of balance is dangerous! The four ways have to live in harmony, as one happy, connected ecosystem. If one way toward number takes over, the ecosystem becomes unstable and some concepts become very difficult for children to learn, for many years to come. For example, many US curricula do not have enough early unitizing and exponentiating. You can observe a huge increase in math failures around the third and fourth grades, when children are faced with problems that depend on groups and units. Don't let it happen to you and yours.

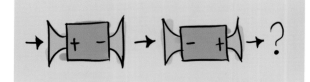

Which math concepts come easier to young children and which are hard? Does it vary from child to child?

We agree with Bruner: "Any subject can be taught effectively in some intellectually honest form to any child at any stage of development." It is not the concepts that are easy or difficult, but how you present them. Help the young kids experience the concept through the whole body and all the senses. For example, mimic one another's poses, cut folded paper, or play with mirrors to explore symmetry. Invite children to answer in actions, rather than words or symbols. For example, a child can prepare enough tires for two toy cars, rather than answer "What is 2x4?" And use technology, because children love it: take photos of kids doing math, record their math stories, search for math pictures and math videos online, use math computer games. You can teach any concept at any age.

How can I stay enthusiastic when my child wants to play the same game again and again, or asks the same question over and over?

Kids get into "vicious cycles": doing something that used to be meaningful again and again with diminishing returns on learning and joy. Kids can never get enough of what they don't really want. Sometimes kids suddenly burst into tears or run away from the game to break the cycle dramatically. Help the kid escape the vicious cycle! Turn it into a spiral leading to new heights. For example, if the kid asks, "Why, why, why?" without paying much attention to answers, make each answer twice as long and detailed as the previous one. And agree to take turns, so you can put in your own, more varied questions. Instead of desperately trying to get some joy out of an old-and-tired game, invite the kid to tweak and redesign its rules. Offer closely related, but different activities.

What is the single best material to have on hand for children to play with math?

We always keep a large stack of graph paper, color pencils or markers, glue, and scissors at the ready. Other than that, we have lots of building toys and construction kits available for both children and adults. Sure, babies may knock your constructions down, but they absorb the ideas anyway. And for sorting, use household or toy objects that are similar, but vary by attributes (color, size, shape) – such as pots and pans, shells, miniature cars, or model animals.

Can young children understand the concept of negative numbers? How should I introduce it?

You can use the opposites to introduce the idea of negative numbers even to a baby. You can put toys on the "underwater elevator" in the bathtub, marking up levels over and under water. Toddlers are happy to play with "objects and anti-objects" that explode, eat, or otherwise cancel one another. For example, three hungry caterpillars can cancel two leaves, but one will stay hungry! In adult talk, -3+2=-1. Pegs (positive numbers) can cancel out holes (negative numbers). If you have three barefoot kids and five socks, how many feet will stay bare? In general, the answer to "Can young children understand the concept of... ?" is always "Yes!"

How old should a child be before I start writing math on paper?

Paper is an excellent cheap medium, and you can use it from birth. At all ages, use pictures and cutouts in addition to symbols. Babies have a grab reflex, so you can put a thick marker into your baby's hand and hold a notepad near enough to the marker's tip for the baby to "draw" for a few seconds. Babies think it's a fun game, and you can always frame the resulting art piece and call it "abstract." Toddlers often enjoy it when they hold a marker, and you hold their hand in yours and draw shapes with it. This develops hand-eye coordination; the hand talks to the brain, and can teach it a thing or two about shapes and symbols!

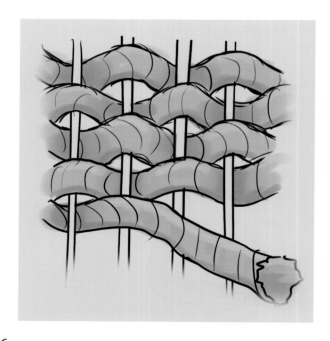

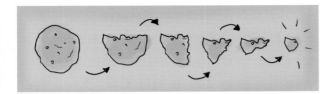

You always talk about adventures and explorations. What about adding numbers fluently, or memorizing multiplication facts?

<u>Make more mundane work meaningful and productive, and track progress</u>. The work is meaningful when the child has deep personal reasons to perform "grind" tasks. Children's personal reasons come down to play, beauty, community, or utility. Children, like grown-ups, will do rather routine tasks as parts of games, or to create art, or because their friends do that, or because they need the task for something else in life.

To track progress, use simple time and task management tools. How can you help children easily see their progress with a task? For example, computer games track progress with levels, achievements, badges. Stay away from rewards, but track and celebrate milestones.

To stay productive, you need good workflow and healthy work habits. Eat before or during math time (math is hungry work), run or jump for a bit before any memorizing (so the brain has enough oxygen), find best time of the day for math (kids know, just ask them), use music or total quiet (depends on the person), and so on.

How can my family get into the habit of doing a bit of interesting math every day?

There are several easy tools you can use. All of them either remind you to do something little, right now – or help you prepare those little math activities for the future.

- Put <u>math art</u> around your house and car, for conversation starters. Change it once in a while.
- Write <u>math graffiti</u> on your walls (or on removable papers) – beautiful words like "fractal" or beautiful symbols like ∞.
- <u>Strew</u> little mathy objects and manipulatives around. Mini-puzzles such as Traffic Jam, small objects for sorting, a card game, construction kits, origami paper – any object that says, "Grab me and do some math!"
- Tie math time to other <u>daily routines</u>. For example, read some math stories before bedtime, or play guessing games while waiting for the bus.
- Once in a month or so, <u>reflect</u> on all the above – get some new math words, math pictures, math objects, and think of your math routines! For ideas, chat with friends who have kids of similar ages and interests.

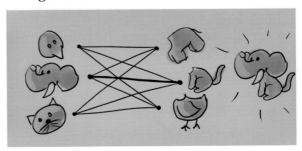

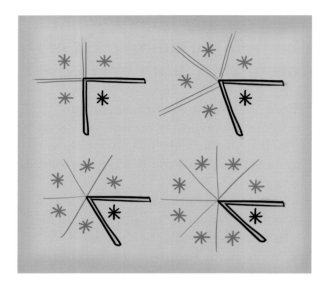

But seriously, can you teach any concept at any age? Can you teach a toddler something like the transitive property?

Oh, a challenge! Try playing "Rock, paper, scissors." It illustrates lack of transitivity very nicely. Also, experiment with storytelling: "If I sit on a chair, and the chair stands on the floor, does it mean I sit on the floor?" Use examples when transitivity does work: "Alice is taller than Bob, and Bob is taller than Carol. Does it mean that Alice is taller than Carol?" All order relations – "heavier" and "faster" and "longer" – are transitive. Toddlers love to sort and order things. Take, for example, the dishes: if the saucer fits into a pan, and the pan fits into a pot, then the saucer will fit into the pot as well. And yes, you can and should use the word "transitive" while playing such games, and your toddler will pick it up. Eventually.

How do I make math manipulatives and game props without spending all my spare time on this?

The medium is the message. In this case, the making of manipulatives is the math. If you can't make it together with the kid, as a part of math explorations, don't make it at all. Designing and making manipulatives is where math is at! Keep even the littlest baby on your knee when you make math pictures or mobiles for him or her, and you will see precious reactions and interest. DIY – Do It Yourself – strongly supports a child's love and understanding of math, but only if "yourself" refers to the child.

Pose your questions and help others at our online Q&A hub:

ask.moebiusnoodles.com

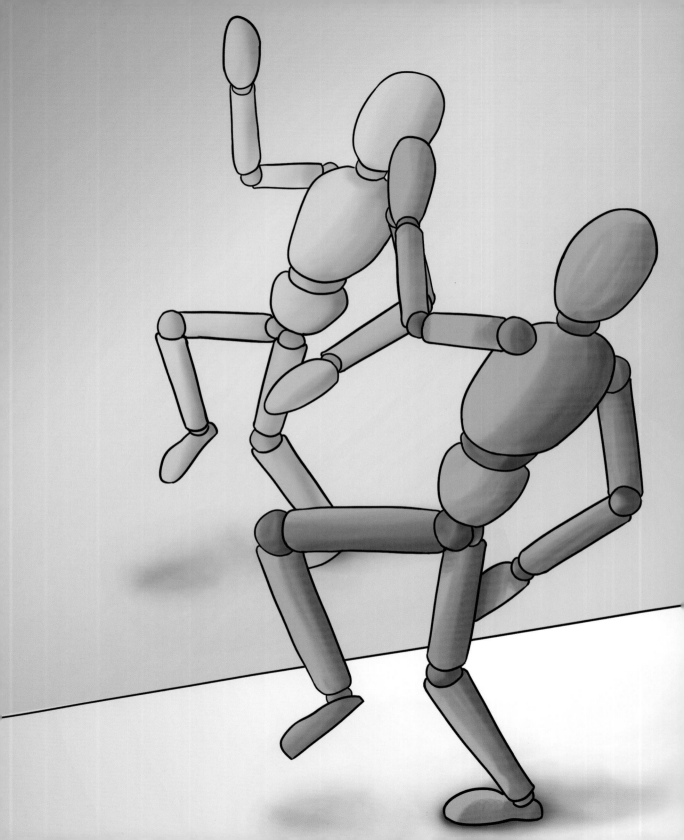

Stand in front of each other and mimic each other's gestures and expressions. That's it! Sounds too easy? As soon as you try crisscross poses, asymmetric finger shapes, or fast motions, the game provides enough challenge even for an adult! You can easily adjust the difficulty to match each child's gross and fine motor skills, as well as attentiveness to details.

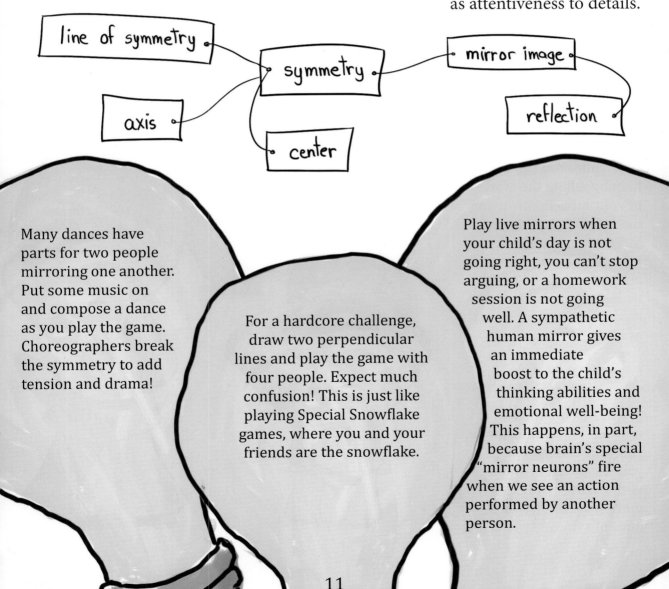

line of symmetry

axis

symmetry

center

mirror image

reflection

Many dances have parts for two people mirroring one another. Put some music on and compose a dance as you play the game. Choreographers break the symmetry to add tension and drama!

For a hardcore challenge, draw two perpendicular lines and play the game with four people. Expect much confusion! This is just like playing Special Snowflake games, where you and your friends are the snowflake.

Play live mirrors when your child's day is not going right, you can't stop arguing, or a homework session is not going well. A sympathetic human mirror gives an immediate boost to the child's thinking abilities and emotional well-being! This happens, in part, because brain's special "mirror neurons" fire when we see an action performed by another person.

Find finger positions and interesting movements that challenge children. Help kids who get confused by mimicking them in return, or gently positioning their limbs with your hands. Ponder why some motions are harder to mimic than others.

Let your baby lead. Follow by mirroring the baby's gestures and facial expressions. Holding the baby in your lap, mirror someone else's gestures by moving baby's hands or feet.

Offer whole body or limb movements, rather than fine gestures. Help with more challenging movements by positioning your child. You can also help by telling the story of your movements using math words: up/down, forward/backward, front/back, perpendicular, across, and so on. Avoid using "left/right" because it confuses in the context of mirrors.

Try more complicated movements – for example, rub your tummy and pat your head. Experiment with friends using two or more "mirrors" (that is, lines of symmetry).

Instead of your own bodies, manipulate dolls, plush toys, models made from construction sets, or posable action figures. It's a math lesson taught by LEGO®, a Barbie®, and a Transformer®!

Take pictures of your games – this will inspire kids to strike more interesting poses! If you take pictures from the side, with the symmetry line in the middle, you can cut them in half and play a matching game with the pieces.

Add objects to the game – give each player a ball, a hula hoop, a large wooden block, or something you can climb. Objects can help kids notice and discuss the idea that "my right is your left."

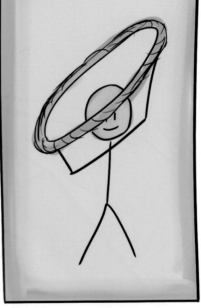

Go on scavenger hunts for characters striking mirror poses or doing copycat movements in games, cartoons, paintings, or dances. Directors, choreographers, and artists use symmetry to express both harmony and conflict. For example, mirrored confrontation shots often appear on posters for action movies.

DOUBLE DOODLE ZOO

Fold a piece of paper in two. Make a random doodle in such a way that it overlaps the fold line – otherwise, the result will fall apart. Now comes the fun part: invite your game partner to see something in the doodle! Add features to it and draw details to make the image more apparent. Cut out the result and open it. Turn the paper over, see something else in the opened shape, and draw the details to make it apparent!

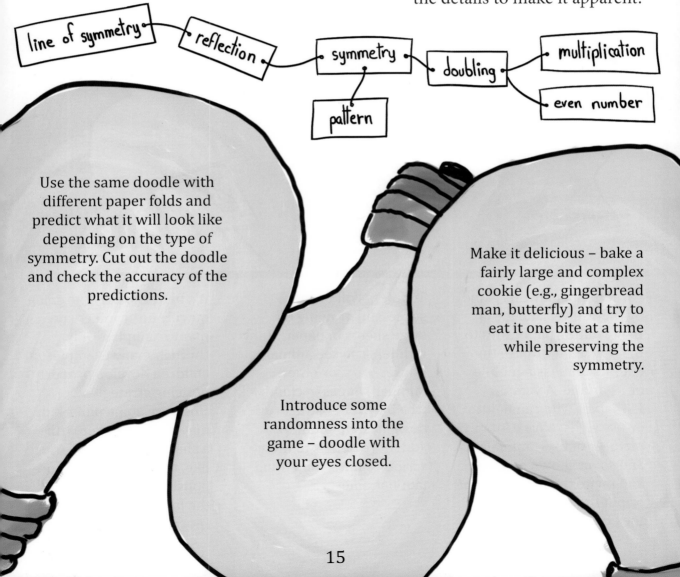

line of symmetry • reflection • symmetry • doubling • multiplication

symmetry • pattern

doubling • even number

Use the same doodle with different paper folds and predict what it will look like depending on the type of symmetry. Cut out the doodle and check the accuracy of the predictions.

Make it delicious – bake a fairly large and complex cookie (e.g., gingerbread man, butterfly) and try to eat it one bite at a time while preserving the symmetry.

Introduce some randomness into the game – doodle with your eyes closed.

Observe kids growing their math eyes as they notice more and more key points, angles, symmetries, quantities, and other mathematical features. Pay attention to these features yourself when it is your turn to see something in the doodle, say their names out loud, and otherwise encourage looking for properties.

Parents can play this game by themselves and give the resulting paper toys to the baby. You can use the cutouts to make a mobile or a garland. A version for babies who can point or use signs: have a lot of pictures of toys, animals, and so on shown at once, and invite the baby to point or put the doodle next to the object it resembles.

Toddlers will be more successful drawing on large sheets of paper. Many toddlers can see animals, houses, cars, or other familiar shapes in clouds, tree bark, or abstract rug designs. Help toddlers add more details to their scribbles until something familiar emerges.

It's better to play the game quickly until you create many examples. Only through many examples do children develop property-noticing strategies. However, some older kids may want to tinker with a shape they particularly like, turning it into a more polished project, such as the Japanese art of Notan (positive-negative space).

Fold the paper into more than two parts. Observe what changes.

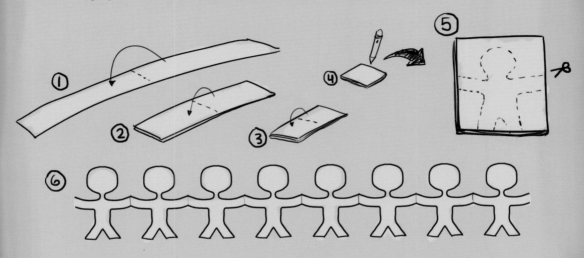

Play this game in reverse – give a child a cutout of a shape or a doodle and suggest to fold along its line (or lines) of symmetry, if any.

Use paint instead of pencil or marker. Paint or just drop paint on paper then fold. Resulting color mixing will add beautiful details to the game.

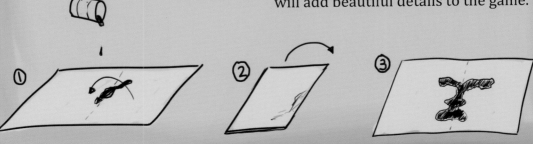

MIRROR BOOK

Lay two plain rectangular mirrors on top of one another, face to face. Connect them at one edge with duct tape. You can usually find small mirrors in dollar stores and school supply or craft stores, and larger mirror tiles in home improvement stores. Put interesting things – like favorite toys or your face – inside the open mirror book. Change the angle between the mirrors and admire the greatest show in math!

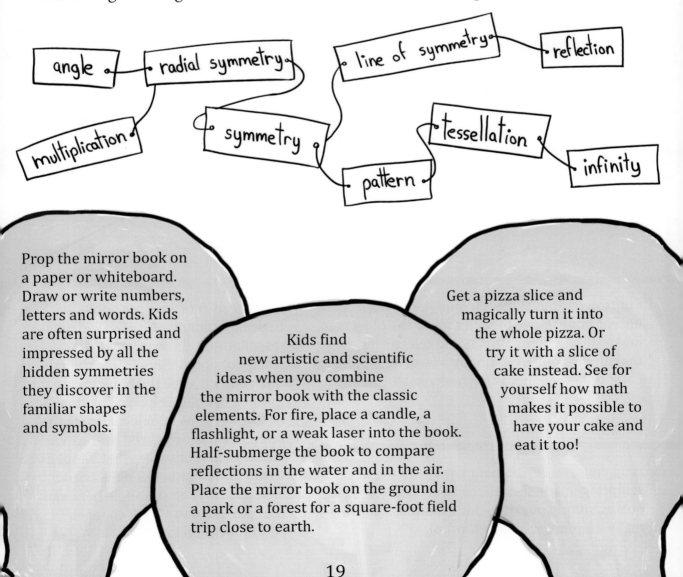

Prop the mirror book on a paper or whiteboard. Draw or write numbers, letters and words. Kids are often surprised and impressed by all the hidden symmetries they discover in the familiar shapes and symbols.

Kids find new artistic and scientific ideas when you combine the mirror book with the classic elements. For fire, place a candle, a flashlight, or a weak laser into the book. Half-submerge the book to compare reflections in the water and in the air. Place the mirror book on the ground in a park or a forest for a square-foot field trip close to earth.

Get a pizza slice and magically turn it into the whole pizza. Or try it with a slice of cake instead. See for yourself how math makes it possible to have your cake and eat it too!

As children play with the mirror book over days and weeks, observe how they make more and more accurate predictions of positions, angles, and shapes. Help children notice radial symmetry in nature: place the center of the mirror book over centers of live flowers, photos of starfish or radiolarians, or models of snowflake and crystals.

Put toys or your fingers inside the opened mirror book. Move the mirrors or the objects to make simple "animations" and tell stories. Move the mirror book over a baby's favorite picture book or family photos for funky kaleidoscope effects.

Help children experiment with drawing or sculpting inside the mirror book. Take turns posing simple puzzles – for example, "Can you make a square with one toothpick?"

Use one or more mirror books to design tiling patterns called tessellations: draw or make a fragment of the tiling inside the mirror book and observe the book taking it to infinity. Encourage your child to place or draw groups of objects inside the book – two shoes, three bears, four wheels – and observe what happens to the total number of objects and reflections when the angle between the "pages" of the book changes (multiplication tables).

Put two mirror books next to each other to form a square "room" with mirror walls. Look inside from the top, to find infinity. Next, try a triangular mirror room – does it work the same?

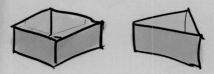

Find all multiplication tables hidden in the mirror book. Open it ninety degrees for times four, seventy-two degrees for times five, sixty degrees for times six, or just count reflections. Even three-year-olds can intuitively find (if not necessarily measure) the angles that turn one toy into three toys, or four toys, in the mirror book.

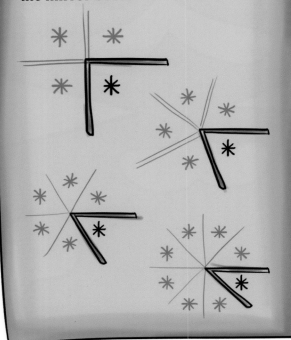

Draw a line across the opening of the mirror book and start closing the book. Your line will form polygons with more and more sides. If you manage to make the opening in the mirror book infinitely small, your polygon will turn into a circle! As with all other ideas that relate to infinity, kids and grown-ups find this deeply meaningful. The idea that polygons approximate circles as the number of sides grows inspired authors of several math adventure books, such as the classic "Flatland" and "The Greedy Triangle."

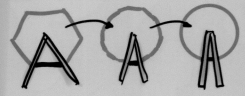

Where in science and technology are angles of mirrors important? Help the child change angles of car mirrors. Look inside physical or virtual telescopes and microscopes. Ask a dentist to explain how mirrors help to see inside the mouth. Watch a video about solar sails.

SPECIAL SNOWFLAKE

Fold a piece of paper through its center repeatedly, then sketch and cut out a snowflake. Coffee filters work well for snowflakes. Giant paper is a lot of fun. Children who can't cut yet can draw or point out shapes of cuts.

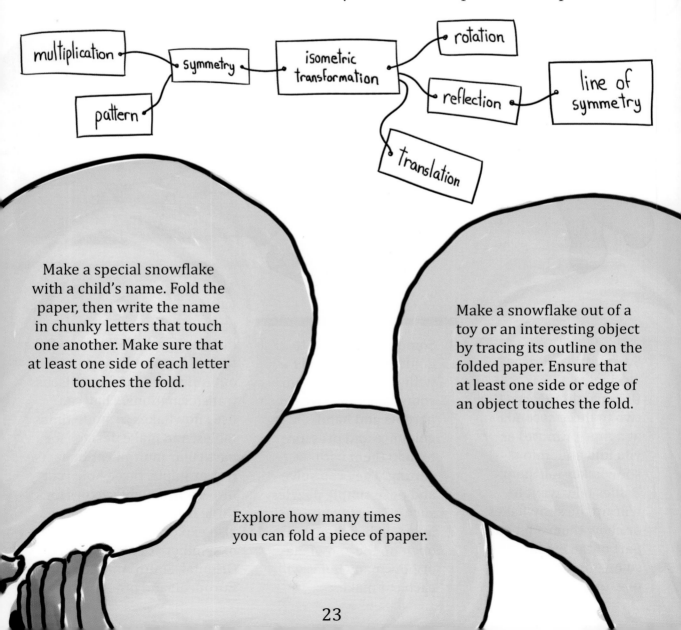

multiplication — symmetry — isometric transformation — rotation

pattern — symmetry

isometric transformation — reflection — line of symmetry

isometric transformation — translation

Make a special snowflake with a child's name. Fold the paper, then write the name in chunky letters that touch one another. Make sure that at least one side of each letter touches the fold.

Make a snowflake out of a toy or an interesting object by tracing its outline on the folded paper. Ensure that at least one side or edge of an object touches the fold.

Explore how many times you can fold a piece of paper.

Vary the number of folds and try trickier six – and ten – layer folds. Keep in mind that children frequently forget where the center of the paper was and fold every which way, with unpredictable results. Celebrate their accidental discoveries and figure out new patterns, but also help them achieve patterns they wanted in the first place.

Symmetric patterns fascinate babies. Observe them focus (for two to three seconds at a time or more) as you fold and unfold snowflakes for them. Babies may want to tear up the snowflakes or chew them a bit as a part of the exploration, so be prepared to make new ones quickly!

Some toddlers like to guide parents' hands with scissors to design snowflakes, or have parents add hand guidance and pressure to help them with cutting. They can solve and pose simple puzzles, such as what shape each hole will be when you open up the snowflake, or how many holes will each cut make.

As children continue working with snowflakes, they can make particular shapes appear at different parts of the snowflake (rhombus, oval, flower), figure out different folds, and discuss transformations. They can use snowflakes to study times tables, and make designs for particular multiplication facts (for example, three holes cut into each of eight sectors for three times eight). They can also explore the arts and crafts of symmetric cutting from Oriental, South American, European and other cultures.

THE SNOWFLAKE'S BASICS

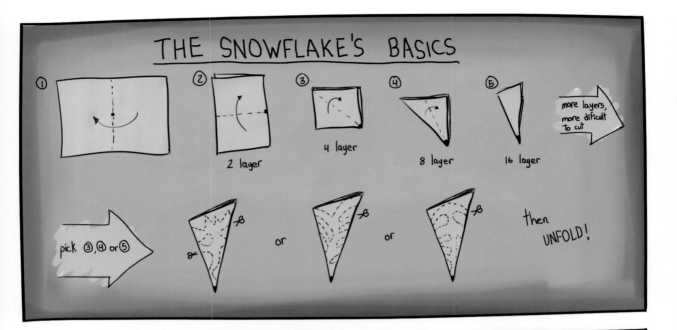

① ② 2 layer ③ 4 layer ④ 8 layer ⑤ 16 layer

more layers, more dificult to cut

pick ③,④ or ⑤

or   or

then UNFOLD!

Challenge one another to create particular folds or cut out particular shapes. Can you make a square in the middle of the snowflake, or a star at its side?

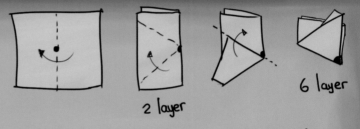

2 layer   6 layer

Make snowflakes with four, five, six, seven, or eight sectors. Use these snowflakes to model times tables.

Try reverse engineering – cut a shape or a letter/number out of unfolded sheet of paper. Let the child explore its line of symmetry (if any) and make predictions as to how folded paper has to be cut to result in the given shape. Test her predictions.

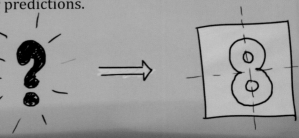

TWO-HAND MIRROR DRAWING

Fold a piece of paper in two or draw a vertical line through the middle. Tape the paper to the table, because your child will draw with both hands, holding a marker in each. Imagine that the middle line is a "mirror." Explain to your child that hands should move symmetrically at every moment – at the same distance, speed and direction from the middle line.

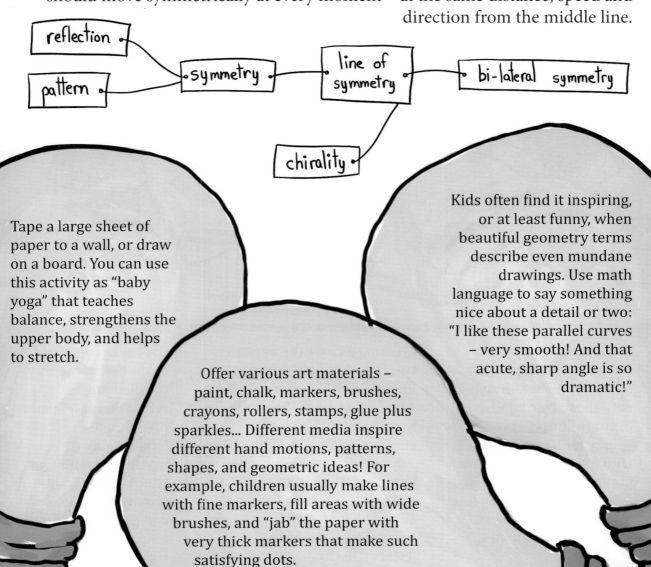

reflection

pattern

symmetry

line of symmetry

bi-lateral symmetry

chirality

Tape a large sheet of paper to a wall, or draw on a board. You can use this activity as "baby yoga" that teaches balance, strengthens the upper body, and helps to stretch.

Kids often find it inspiring, or at least funny, when beautiful geometry terms describe even mundane drawings. Use math language to say something nice about a detail or two: "I like these parallel curves – very smooth! And that acute, sharp angle is so dramatic!"

Offer various art materials – paint, chalk, markers, brushes, crayons, rollers, stamps, glue plus sparkles... Different media inspire different hand motions, patterns, shapes, and geometric ideas! For example, children usually make lines with fine markers, fill areas with wide brushes, and "jab" the paper with very thick markers that make such satisfying dots.

Gently pose problems and challenges (for example, "Make a symmetric house"). If kids draw something that is not a reflection, replace the middle line with a real mirror. Ask them to trace the element again with the dominant hand, and observe what "the hand in the mirror" does – and how the mirror element looks.

Use large boards, large safe markers, large chalk, or paint brushes, drawing with the baby's hands in yours at first. If your youngster likes playing with food, finger paint with pureed food on a tray – use a noodle as the middle line! Start with the simplest pattern – vertical lines.

Creating a circle (face) from two halves, with the symmetry line through the center, looks simple, but it is a challenging beginner puzzle. Think of simple shapes approximating symmetric objects kids love. For example, make a rocket out of a rectangle and a triangle, or a cat out of a circle and two triangles. Do the kid's favorite letters have line symmetry?

Use more complex shapes with spirals (challenging to reflect) and elements of different sizes (challenging to match well with two hands). Pose goals requiring analysis and prediction: draw a square, a triangle, a right triangle.

Invite your child to finger-paint in a plate or tray covered with gel or granular material: wet sand, shaving cream, or rice. The tactile pleasure of the material and the intellectual challenge of the symmetry combine into a very engaging task.

Go beyond painting and turn the game into a musical experience. Set up two xylophones, turned so they mirror each other. Or create your own mirror percussion stand out of two lines of identical cups, bottles, and pots.

Take two small cars and dip their wheels into paint. Hand the cars over to your child, stand back and get ready to be amazed at the intricate symmetrical curves that come from "racing" cars around!

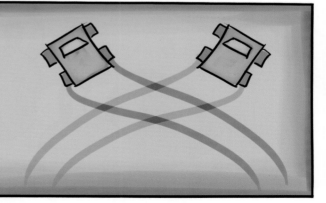

ONE-TWO-THREE AND MORE

One fish, two fish... It is very easy, but not very interesting, to make a collection of random objects in any quantity. The real challenge comes from finding many numbers in the same story or context. In this game, children's creativity, their divergent thinking, and their love of delectable detail can brilliantly shine! Let's try finding quantities that are icons for recognizing well-known objects, stories and contexts. In the Goldilock and the three bears story, for example, there is one Goldilock; the bears' house has two rooms; three is obvious; four can be bear paws or chair legs. Can you find five, six, and other quantities hidden in the story and the illustrations?

Science and math behind iconic quantities can go deep enough to interest teens and adults. For example, natural minerals cannot form five-sided crystal prisms, but five is a very frequent quantity in the living nature. There is even a giraffe with five horns!

Animal legs come in pairs. Use them for an iconic collection about even numbers. Fairy tales usually have a lot of odd numbers, with three and seven most popular.

Numbers often have historical, cultural, or mythological significance. Looking for iconic quantities can lead to wild virtual journeys across continents and through time. Invite kids to meet the four sons of Horus in Egypt, the nine muses in Ancient Greece, or the 108 Hindu deities.

Make a counting book about your favorite story or topic. It's a pleasant art project, and a way to share your interests with kids. If you need inspiration, check out "The Book of Threes" at www.threes.com

Make collections about topics the baby loves. Use the same method for each collection to point out quantities. For example, put sticky notes on toy truck's wheels, each of the three bears in the book, or baby's own two feet. Name small quantities without counting, because babies can instantly distinguish quantities up to five (subitizing).

Make a photo counting book about your child playing with iconic quantities. Children love to look at themselves working on something. It is hard to find many quantities in the same context, and young children may not care about this aspect of the activity. If your child finds an example from another context, just start one more collection.

It may be very hard to find some numbers in a given context. There may be a reason worth exploring! For example, you can make an excellent counting book out of animal legs, as long as you stay with even numbers, because animals have line symmetry.

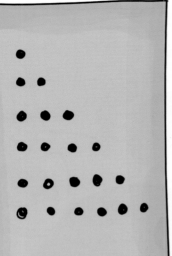

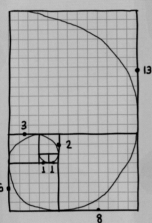

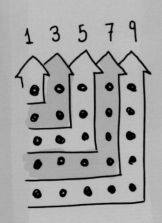

Investigate not only the counting sequence one, two, three... but other sequences – for example, even numbers two, four, six, eight... (cars and trucks, anyone?) or Fibonacci numbers one, one, two, three, five, eight, thirteen.. (great for nature walks!) Nursery rhymes often have countdown sequences starting with "ten little..."

You can make a mobile "counting sculpture" to display your collection of iconic objects. Some numbers are easier to find and display in 3D, such as the six faces of a cube.

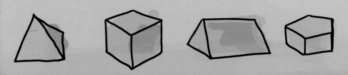

The hunt for iconic quantities and sequences can become addictive! Whether you go grocery shopping or travel to a galaxy far, far away in books, movies, and computer games, you will find iconic quantities hidden in vegetables, spaceships, or alien life-forms. How about creating your own fantasy island or sci-fi universe centered on your favorite number sequence?

SuperAutoSimilarly-Fractoalidocious

Sketch an object or shape your child likes. We will call that shape "the base." What iconic quantity does the base show? To find out, mark the points that stick out, such as the tips of cats' ears (two), vertices of a triangle (three), or ends of a star (five). Draw smaller versions of the base at each of the marked points. Mark the same points on each of the smaller versions, and draw even smaller versions of the base at each of these points. Repeat the process as many times as you want. You just made several levels of a fractal! This type is called tree fractal.

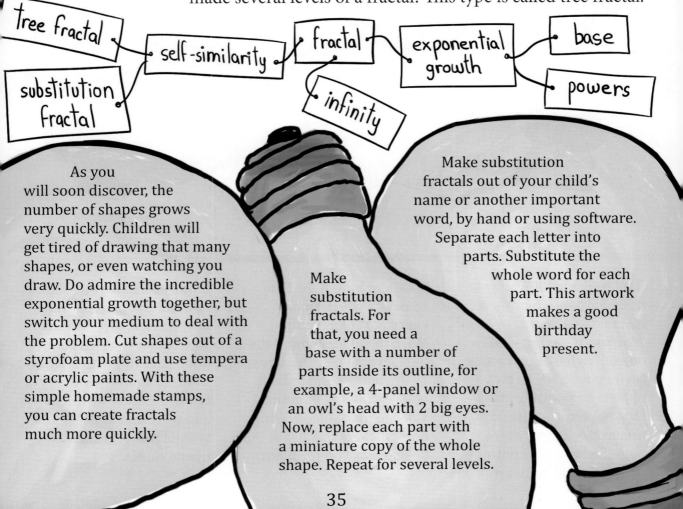

tree fractal

self-similarity

fractal

exponential growth

base

substitution fractal

infinity

powers

As you will soon discover, the number of shapes grows very quickly. Children will get tired of drawing that many shapes, or even watching you draw. Do admire the incredible exponential growth together, but switch your medium to deal with the problem. Cut shapes out of a styrofoam plate and use tempera or acrylic paints. With these simple homemade stamps, you can create fractals much more quickly.

Make substitution fractals. For that, you need a base with a number of parts inside its outline, for example, a 4-panel window or an owl's head with 2 big eyes. Now, replace each part with a miniature copy of the whole shape. Repeat for several levels.

Make substitution fractals out of your child's name or another important word, by hand or using software. Separate each letter into parts. Substitute the whole word for each part. This artwork makes a good birthday present.

Help children sustain the fractal structure. Provide tools such as stamps, as well as your drawing and paper-cutting services, to make repetition easier for kids. Explore the ethnomathematics of fractals, such as African patterns.

Babies like to look at fractal art and to observe its making. Use their favorite characters and objects as bases of fractals. Invite your baby to pick objects by pointing at toys or pictures. Use touchscreen devices to help the baby play with simple fractal software.

Toddlers have hard time remembering to make every part of a picture. Mark the places where the next level of pictures goes, or invite the child to do it before drawing or gluing. You can mark places with dots, stickers or raisins – to be eaten as you progress!

Children can predict the number of objects at the next level, and pose and solve other puzzles about quantities in fractals. Offer children to use software to make digital fractals, and to design large-scale artistic projects such as fractal quilts.

Bake fractal cookies! Simple geometric shapes and substitution fractals are easiest to make, but experiment with different shapes. These are popular treats on math holidays such as Pi Day or Sonya Kovalevsky Day.

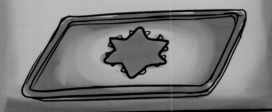

Make a fractal collage out of found objects, such as leaves of different sizes. You can also cut many copies of the base shape at once, out of folded thin paper. Recycle magazines for random splashes of different colors within similar shapes that make a fractal.

Read stories about fractals and draw pictures for them. The hydra grew two heads when Hercules cut out one – can you imagine what that looked like, some time into the fight? The hydra story is about powers of two. An Indian legend about the inventor of chess asking for one grain of rice on the first square of the chessboard, two on the second, four on the third, and so on, is about powers of two as well. "When I was going to St. Ives" is a poem about powers of seven. It can be traced back to a five-thousand-year old homework problem, found on an Egyptian tablet.

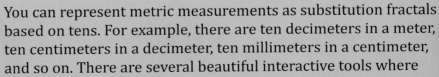

You can represent metric measurements as substitution fractals based on tens. For example, there are ten decimeters in a meter, ten centimeters in a decimeter, ten millimeters in a centimeter, and so on. There are several beautiful interactive tools where you can zoom in and out through the powers of ten, exploring sizes of objects in our Universe.

THE BIG HUNT FOR QUANTITIES

Look for iconic quantities in nature or culture. There are all sorts! Find quantities so small you can subitize them at a glance, or so large you will grow old before you finish counting. Investigate quantities that come in sets, collections, and groups of groups that represent multiplication. What quantities can you discover in self-similar, fractal structures?

You can start by looking in the mirror. Ask questions such as "What do we usually have one of? Two of?" Continue the scavenger hunt around the house and out in the yard. Take photos or make sketches of your finds.

quantity · subitizing · counting · multiplication · exponentiation · number

iconic quantity

Play "Imagine That!" by making silly changes to iconic quantities and groups, and telling stories of what happens. Imagine that... a teapot has two spouts! Imagine that... your hand has little hands on each fingertip! Imagine that... we have no coins or bills other than pennies! As they play, children seek out fun iconic quantities, and analyze the roles of quantities in different situations.

Pick a quantity and find many different ways to arrive at it. For example, you can draw twelve objects as two groups of six (an egg carton), as three groups of four (claws of a sloth), or as ten and two. You can arrive at sixteen by two different power paths: it's four of fours, but also two of twos of twos of twos! Sort quantities by types of paths that lead to them. For example, you can only arrive at numbers like seven, eleven, and nineteen (primes) by addition, not by multiplication or exponentiation!

Since the ancient times, people have been designing tools and toys with subitizing in mind. Dice, dominoes, playing cards, abacus, even some number systems (Roman and Mayan, for example) use easily recognizable groups of symbols. Can you find these and other examples of groups of small quantities in everyday objects? Keep in mind that we are so used to many of these examples that we overlook them easily!

Searching for special numbers in nature has long traditions in many cultures, with mixed-bag results from beautiful geometry of the Pythagoreans to quackery such as numerology. Help children find beauty and fun in iconic quantities – without giving too much weight to random coincidences!

Babies can subitize at birth, and have rather impressive powers of pattern recognition. Make collections of different designs with the same visual pattern: six dots as they are on a die, five marks as they are on the playing card, and so on.

Toddlers can go on scavenger hunts themselves, either for a given iconic quantity, or for all quantities they can find in a room or a park. Help them photograph or sketch. Invite kids to play matching and sorting games with their pictures. For example, you can make a set of cards for the game "Memory," with each matched pair showing the same quantity with different objects.

Older children enjoy finding their favorite numbers everywhere and expanding their notion of numbers with beauties such as the golden mean or Pi. They can also hunt for interesting ways to represent number properties, such as solving "The ants are marching one by one..." puzzle with manipulatives.

You can find iconic quantities as key elements in fiction, such as "Three Billy Goats Gruff" or "The Good, the Bad, and the Ugly." Children will also love scientific or engineering stories about iconic quantities. For example, two eyes are required for binocular vision, which helps the survival of animals. The three legs of a tripod is a minimum number for stable inanimate objects, while creatures (or robots) who move to keep their balance can stand on two legs.

Ponder why so many things in fairy tales, myths, and jokes come in threes and sevens. After building a large collection of examples, ask children to think about it for a few days. Write down all their ideas and explore mathematics behind them. For example, three is the first natural number that people consider "many" – with sayings in many languages such as "three is a crowd." Seven is the first prime number beyond the subitizing range. You can't split seven into equal groups, so it seems challenging and even mysterious. Don't rush these investigations all at once, but pay more attention to numbers in stories and sayings.

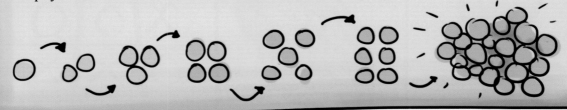

Explore iconic quantities through music and dance. Can two stand for polka, three for waltz, four for blues, because their time signatures are 2/4, 3/4, and 4/4? How about quantities in musical intervals, harmonies, and chords?

REAL MULTIPLICATION TABLES

Your mission, should you choose to accept it, is to find and build groups of identical collections. Both the number of objects per collection, and the number of collections in the group, must be iconic numbers. For example, there are sixteen chess pieces on each of the two sides of the board – an iconic two-by-sixteen. The four seasons each have three months for an iconic three-by-four. Cerberus the three-headed dog had two-by-three eyes.

multiplication table — multiplication — iconic quantity — group — unitizing

Iconic multiplication comes in ways other than groups of groups. Find iconic areas – for example, in a two-by-four board, or a four-by-six photograph. Hunt for iconic arrays, such as egg cartons (two-by-five or two-by-six) and chess boards (eight-by-eight). Find units of units in measurements, such as three-by-twelves inches per yard, or ten-by-ten millimeters in a decimeter.

Ask friends, family members, or professionals in fields your child loves about their special examples of multiplication. You can learn a lot about professions – and people! A space engineer can tell you each of the five space shuttles designed by NASA required two solid rocket boosters plus an external tank with liquid fuel for an iconic five-by-three. A grandma who always knits mittens for her four grandkids' winter holiday gift has to make two-by-four. A country singer will think of the six strings and nineteen frets on the classic guitar.

Prepare an empty grid and a stack of index cards. Each time you notice an iconic multiplication example, sketch it on a card and put it into the corresponding cell. Some combinations are easier to find than others, so you can have multiple cards in the same cell. Decide what to do about the symmetric times facts (for example, two-by-five and five-by-two).

It's pretty hard to find examples for numbers greater than five. You may find the hunt for intrinsic multiplication strangely addictive. Enjoy the challenge!

Put up pictures on walls, or create your own book with dots or stickers highlighting what you count in each illustration. Photograph the baby holding objects representing iconic quantities.

If the examples toddlers find aren't quite iconic, accept them anyway. The point is to find multiplication, not to argue whether the quantities are always the same. Pay special attention to twos and fives. A toddler can use fingers to match a group of five. This happy familiarity helps with our decimal (two fives!) system.

Once examples are collected, children can create an artistic multiplication poster in a consistent style. Invite kids to try timed or competitive scavenger hunts, with challenges to photograph as many iconic multiplication examples at a museum or a park as they can.

Some children like to relax the iconic requirement and make times tables out of their favorite object, grouped many times. For example, a kid will group two evening primrose flowers with four petals each for two-by-four, then three flowers for three-by-four, and so on.

Can you find iconic addition? This is harder than finding multiplication! For example, car stickers show people in the family, such as two adults plus one child equals three family members.

Explore coins and bills of different countries. For example, in the US, twenty nickels or ten dimes or four quarters make a dollar: twenty-by-five equals ten-by-ten equals four-by-twenty-five equals one hundred.

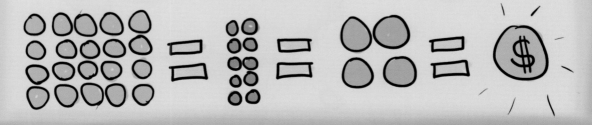

FUNCTION MACHINE

Sketch or build a "function machine" that takes objects in and then transforms them. Make up a rule your kid will be able to guess, but not immediately. Let the kid put in objects or numbers a few times to see what happens to them and to guess the transformation rule.

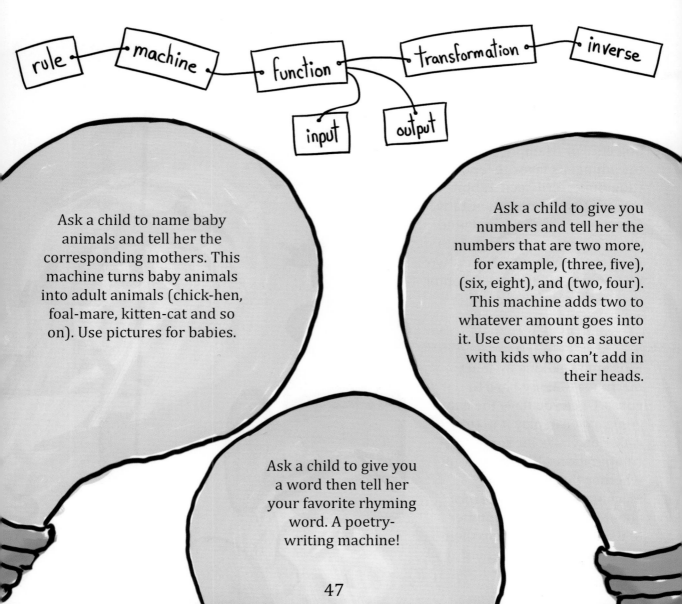

rule • machine • function • transformation • inverse

input output

Ask a child to name baby animals and tell her the corresponding mothers. This machine turns baby animals into adult animals (chick-hen, foal-mare, kitten-cat and so on). Use pictures for babies.

Ask a child to give you numbers and tell her the numbers that are two more, for example, (three, five), (six, eight), and (two, four). This machine adds two to whatever amount goes into it. Use counters on a saucer with kids who can't add in their heads.

Ask a child to give you a word then tell her your favorite rhyming word. A poetry-writing machine!

47

Help children stay consistent with their machine's rules. Use spreadsheets: program a formula you or older kids invent, hide the formula, let others guess the formula from inputs and outputs. Help children organize scavenger hunts for functions in stories or everyday surroundings.

Use qualitative functions – that is, machines that work without numbers. How about a machine that adds a sticker to each toy thrown into it by a baby, or a machine that finds each baby animal's mommy?

Invite toddlers to change the first object and then repeat that same operation on other objects. For example, give each toy animal its favorite food (dog-bone, bird-seed, rabbit-carrot). Use simple quantitative functions such as the machine doubling whatever enters into it, or giving every character two raisins to eat. So, if several enter, you need to prepare enough raisins.

Kids enjoy making up fancy machines that are hard to guess. Once you have the game going, you can play it in the car or on walks for some oral computations. Kids may argue whether the guess, "The machine doubles," is correct about their "Add the number to itself" function – help them figure out what's going on!

Build a machine that gives each animal a house. Check out the book, "A House Is a House for Me."

Find function machines in daily life (washer, toaster, microwave oven).

Look for magical machines in fairy tales (hint: they transform objects and people or grant wishes).

WALK AROUND IN CIRCLES

Choose a function you like. Connect the function machine's output with its input to create a loop. Apply the function again, and again, and again… See what happens!

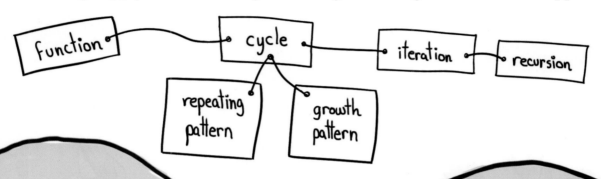

Many stories have loops or iterations of the same action. Read stories about the circle of life, rebirth and regrowth, or grains of rice that double again and again from one square of the chessboard to the next, or cumulative tales where the action repeats with an escalation, like "The Gingerbread Man".

Cut or break a cookie or a paper square in half, and then cut that half in half again, and again, and again. Have you seen kids doing it with their favorite food to savor it longer? How small can you go? Put the pieces back together again – they add up to the original whole piece.

Fold sheets, towels, or just paper together with children – it's a surprisingly engaging activity. Fold in half again and again and again. How small can you make a newspaper page by folding?

51

Help kids repeat the same action reliably, for they tend to forget the rule between iterations or change it whimsically. Keep up the scavenger hunt for iterating functions and repeating cycles in stories, games, or household activities.

Babies like to repeat their favorite actions many, many times. They are naturals at this game! For example, a function machine can add a railroad car to Thomas the Tank Engine® when he passes the station. Assemble the track into a loop and build a really long train!

Place a few toys around a big chair or bed. Walk along this round toy path "visiting" each toy and calling out, drawing, or writing down who you visit. Repeat again and again. Many toddlers love this game and, surprisingly, find it challenging to predict what's next, especially with five to seven toys total – even after many repetitions!

Make a shape out of counters, then make the shape grow, then make it grow again, and again, and again – predictably. Guess how each next step is made out of the previous (the recursive formula). Can you predict 10th or 100th step (the closed formula)?

Come up with a function that brings smaller and smaller results as you repeat it. In economics, when you work more and more to achieve smaller and smaller results, the process is said to have "diminishing returns."

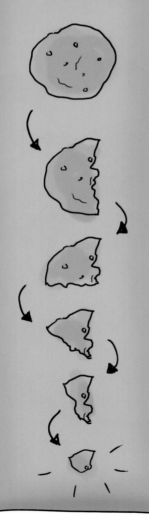

Collect and sort functions by how they iterate. You can iterate some functions forever, for example, doubling or singing "The Bear Went Over the Mountain" song. Some functions only iterate for a while, like breaking a cookie into ever smaller pieces or cutting paper in half repeatedly. Some functions don't iterate at all, or stop changing from iteration to iteration, such as subtracting a number from itself. Invite children to come up with ideas for keeping the iterations going, such as introducing negative numbers or creating a "reset" option.

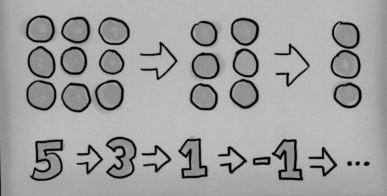

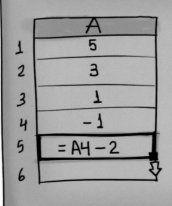

Write a recursive formula in a spreadsheet (for example, A2=A1-2) and drag it down the column. Invite kids to observe and modify the pattern. Like many activities that have to do with cycles, it is more engaging than it sounds from this description.

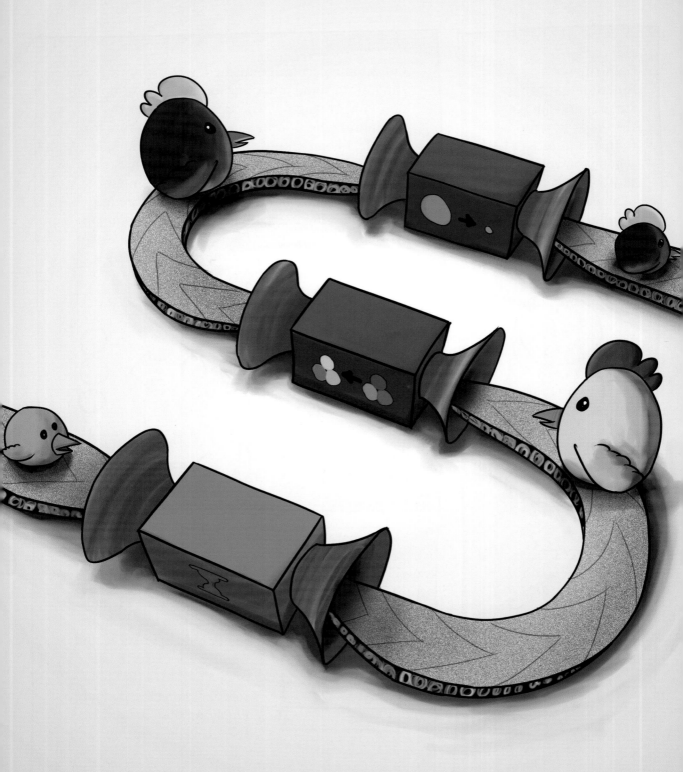

NEW FUNCTIONS FROM OLD

Create or find two function machines. Attach the output of one of them to the input of the other. This is called "composition of functions." Some compositions make perfect sense, some are silly and make you laugh, and some don't work at all, because domains and ranges are incompatible. Try many compositions and see what happens!

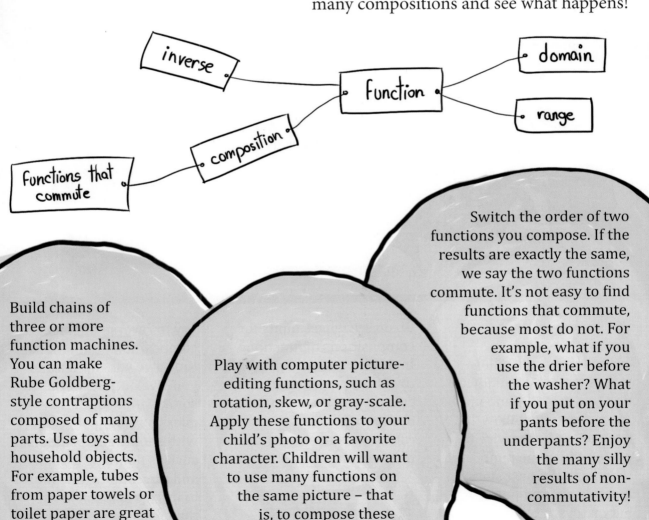

Build chains of three or more function machines. You can make Rube Goldberg-style contraptions composed of many parts. Use toys and household objects. For example, tubes from paper towels or toilet paper are great for marble runs.

Play with computer picture-editing functions, such as rotation, skew, or gray-scale. Apply these functions to your child's photo or a favorite character. Children will want to use many functions on the same picture – that is, to compose these functions!

Switch the order of two functions you compose. If the results are exactly the same, we say the two functions commute. It's not easy to find functions that commute, because most do not. For example, what if you use the drier before the washer? What if you put on your pants before the underpants? Enjoy the many silly results of non-commutativity!

Help children find functions all around! A washer makes dirty clothes clean; an oven makes raw food cooked. Ponder the difference between functions as actions-on-objects and functions as correspondences. For example: an action function doubles the number of legs to make fantastic four-legged chickens; a correspondence function finds mother animals for baby animals, such as hens for chicks. This idea comes up a lot in programming.

Put several "action stations" in a row. For example, the sofa pillow makes the baby, a teddy, a doll (anything!) jump up twice. Go to the pillow, lift a toy or the baby twice to pretend-play the jump, and then go to the next station. A magic box can put a hat on toys, a blanket can invite them to sleep, a plate can feed them, and so on.

Go on scavenger hunts for compositions of functions. In the house: bathing then toweling; peeling then cutting veggies. In books or museums: eggs to caterpillars to chrysalises to butterflies.

Try to reverse-engineer a composition of functions! Kids give you inputs, and you give outputs of the composition, until they guess both functions. Start with simple compositions, such as doubling a number and then adding one more to it. This is much harder than guessing a single machine, and leads to more math discussions.

Explore cumulative tales. They are made of compositions of correspondences:
This is the cat,
That killed the rat,
That ate the malt
That lay in the house that Jack built.

Experiment with musical functions, such as transpositions and changes of volume. For example, kids can sing the same song lower, but louder. Make changes with your voices, or apply functions in sound-editing software to a recording of your voices.

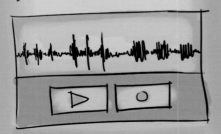

Try to compose a function with its inverse. What happens?

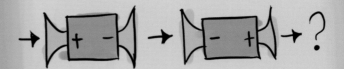

Experiment with composing functions as correspondences and functions as actions. For example, a correspondence function can find animal parents (puppy → dog), or the number of feet the animal has (dog → 4 feet). Compose these with the doubling function (an action): puppy → dog → 4 feet → 8 feet. A dog with eight feet? Drawing that will surprise even a baby!

Think of rules in your favorite board game as functions – for example, the random function of rolling a die. Then change rules by composition and observe what happens to the gameplay. For example, double all die rolls – will the game go faster? Or add spinner rolls to die rolls. Does it matter if you roll the die or spin the spinner first?

SILLY ROBOT

Choose a simple physical task, such as filling a glass with water, or putting on shoes. The "silly robot" should be someone who knows the game well. Robot only understands simple, one-step commands, such as "move forward" or "pick up the glass." The robot is trying as hard as it can to mess up the task, without actually disobeying directions. For example, the child says, "Put the shoe on" and the robot puts it on its hand. The child commands, "Put the glass down" and the robot does, except the glass is sideways and all the water spills out! The goal for the robot is to find funny loopholes, and the goal for the player is to give commands without loopholes.

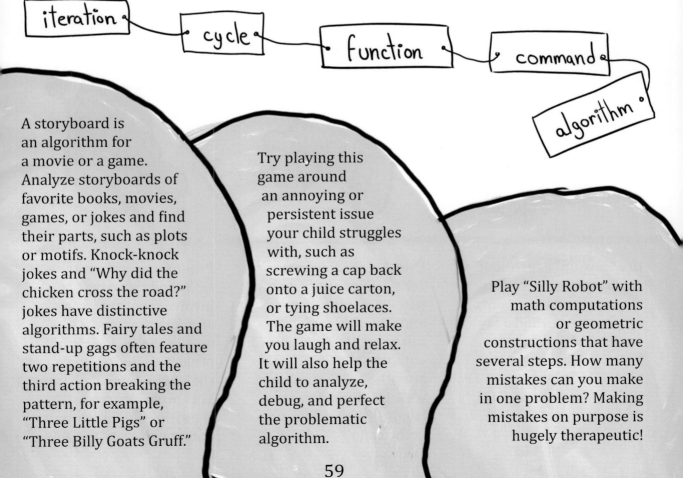

A storyboard is an algorithm for a movie or a game. Analyze storyboards of favorite books, movies, games, or jokes and find their parts, such as plots or motifs. Knock-knock jokes and "Why did the chicken cross the road?" jokes have distinctive algorithms. Fairy tales and stand-up gags often feature two repetitions and the third action breaking the pattern, for example, "Three Little Pigs" or "Three Billy Goats Gruff."

Try playing this game around an annoying or persistent issue your child struggles with, such as screwing a cap back onto a juice carton, or tying shoelaces. The game will make you laugh and relax. It will also help the child to analyze, debug, and perfect the problematic algorithm.

Play "Silly Robot" with math computations or geometric constructions that have several steps. How many mistakes can you make in one problem? Making mistakes on purpose is hugely therapeutic!

59

Help children capture steps in algorithms in some form – silly pictures, words, symbols. Help children to see the mathematical value of precise commands, to reuse and combine good algorithms, and to debug silly ones. Share ways you organize complex, multi-step actions in your life, such as to-do lists, flowcharts, computer programs and so on.

Use "mix-up" gags about routine tasks! Put socks on your hands and pants on your head. Hold a toy cow and claim that it says "Woof" – or point at the baby's belly button and say, "Where is your nose? Is this your nose?"

Even before children are verbal, they use gestures to tell parents what to do and what they want. You can play silly robot games with these "baby signs" after they are established well. Just make sure to laugh with the child, not at the child.

Progress to more complex tasks and those that involve repetition, such as doing the same fold on all sides of an origami project, or decorating a room with several pictures. This promotes reuse of algorithms and their parts – that is, cycles or iterations.

Once a child creates a working algorithm, see if it can be applied to new objects. For example, if the silly robot can fill a glass with water, will the same algorithm work to fill a vase, a pot, a pool, or a tub with water?

Suggest a child finds a way to capture steps from algorithms. This leads to invented notation. Children like inventing their own math symbols – and seeing themselves among historical inventors of math or programming notation, like Ada Lovelace or Leonardo Fibonacci.

Analyze each command – is it hard to explain to a robot or is it easy? What types of commands are hard to explain? Are there tasks that cannot be programmed at all?

MAKE YOUR OWN GRIDS

This activity needs to happen shortly after kids start playing with ready-made grids, or looking at grid art, or otherwise engaging with grids. Simply say: "Can you make a grid?"

Making a grid is more challenging than you may expect. Kids often draw grids cell by cell, and have a hard time keeping the structure. Some kids will probably be stuck. Don't offer help while they are thinking; wait until they ask, however long it takes. If the child asks how to start, hint that a grid can be made by drawing, folding paper, or arranging cards and offer the materials.

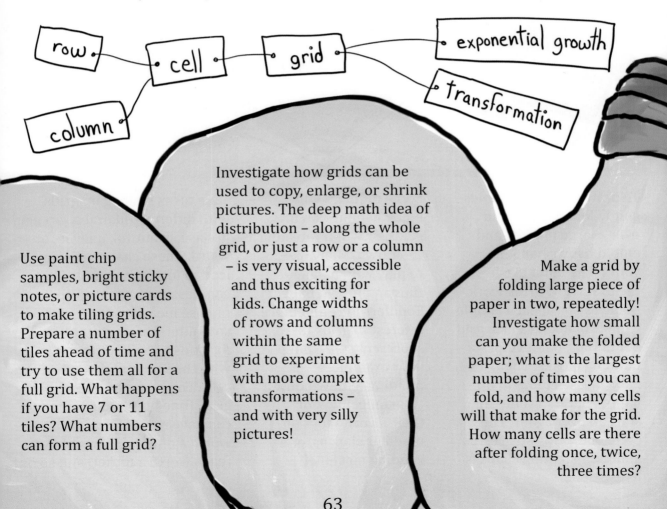

row · cell · grid · exponential growth

column

transformation

Use paint chip samples, bright sticky notes, or picture cards to make tiling grids. Prepare a number of tiles ahead of time and try to use them all for a full grid. What happens if you have 7 or 11 tiles? What numbers can form a full grid?

Investigate how grids can be used to copy, enlarge, or shrink pictures. The deep math idea of distribution – along the whole grid, or just a row or a column – is very visual, accessible and thus exciting for kids. Change widths of rows and columns within the same grid to experiment with more complex transformations – and with very silly pictures!

Make a grid by folding large piece of paper in two, repeatedly! Investigate how small can you make the folded paper; what is the largest number of times you can fold, and how many cells will that make for the grid. How many cells are there after folding once, twice, three times?

Offer help gently, but let children experiment on their own! Investigate how grids are used in art, design, city planning, and other professions, and what tools each profession uses to keep their grids precise and accurate.

To draw grids with babies, gently fold baby's hand over a large marker, and enfold baby's hand in yours. The hand teaches the brain how grids work. Babies also repeat a simple game: you make a nice grid out of tiles, paint chips, or building blocks. Then, the baby messes the grid up, happy that the game can start all over again! The cycle of making structures and then creating chaos is irresistible.

Some toddlers will enjoy helping you make grids, or will try making their own. Many like to play with magnetic tiles and to fold paper. Toddlers may find more interest in grids that represent something – for example, a building with windows, an arrangement of their favorite toys on modular shelves, or a vending machine.

Take turns making up grids with different qualities: circular, precise, beautiful, uneven, or weird. These challenges may lead to interesting tools like compasses and gauges, to precise measurements, and to computer-based explorations. Ask kids to build different grids with the same total number of cells. For example, "one-dollar grid" (one hundred pennies) can have rows of ten (each worth a dime) or rows of five (each worth a nickel) and so on.

Artists often use grids to plan composition. Explore art work that uses regular grids, curved grids, and grids where row and column heights and widths vary. Experiment with changing grid lines to create perspective or to distort images.

Many children enjoy weaving, which is another way of making grids. Build a basic loom and provide a variety of materials for weaving. Research the history, science, and math of traditional weave patterns, and experiment with your own patterns.

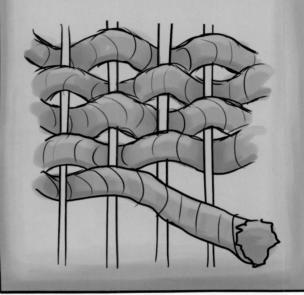

Make funky grid art by arranging painter's tape on a piece of cardboard, or even an old bed sheet or a tee-shirt. Paint over the grid. Once the paint is dry, carefully remove the tape and enjoy your Mondrian-style artwork!

GRIDS AND CHIMERAS

Prepare a grid with large cells. Draw a cat head (or your kid's favorite animal) in each cell of the first column, and a cat body in each cell of the first row. The corner cell will have the whole cat. Ask the child to pick the next animal (babies and toddlers can point at pictures or toys to pick). Draw the head of that animal in each cell of the second column, and the body in each cell of the second row. Kids may want to draw heads and bodies, or have you draw with their hand in yours. Use different colors for different animals. Younger children may want to "drive" a toy truck along rows and columns, "delivering" heads and bodies to each cell.

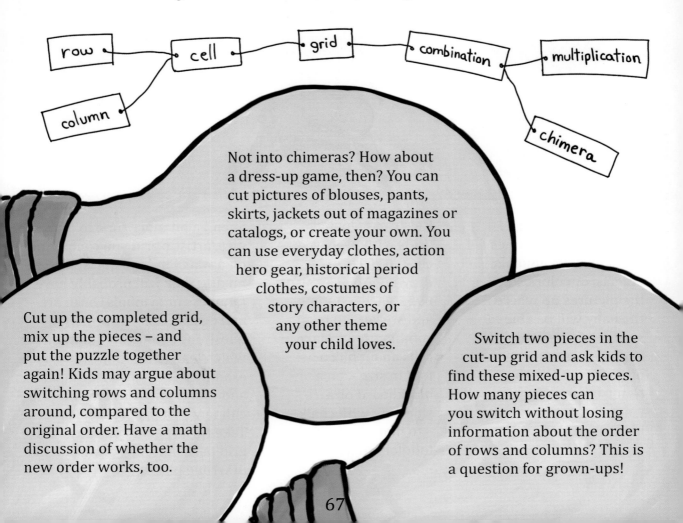

row • • cell • • grid • • combination • • multiplication

column

chimera

Not into chimeras? How about a dress-up game, then? You can cut pictures of blouses, pants, skirts, jackets out of magazines or catalogs, or create your own. You can use everyday clothes, action hero gear, historical period clothes, costumes of story characters, or any other theme your child loves.

Cut up the completed grid, mix up the pieces – and put the puzzle together again! Kids may argue about switching rows and columns around, compared to the original order. Have a math discussion of whether the new order works, too.

Switch two pieces in the cut-up grid and ask kids to find these mixed-up pieces. How many pieces can you switch without losing information about the order of rows and columns? This is a question for grown-ups!

Help kids keep the structure, and bring up famous chimeras and modular structures from mythology or engineering. Kids may get bored drawing similar pictures in many cells, so help them finish grids quickly. Then play with hiding cells, taking grids apart and other puzzles. Find examples of using grids for combinations in everyday and scientific media.

Draw combination grids in front of babies using favorite animals, objects, or colors. Put the pictures up where the baby will be able to see them, for example, in corridors where you often carry the baby. Name combinations as you point at them ("cat-bird" and "bird-cat").

Kids can help make grids with prepared cut-out parts or drawing. You can also use stencils, stamps, and stickers to form combinations. Make cells about half a foot in size – on a blackboard or a sidewalk with chalk – to make it easier for toddlers to draw.

Spend a bit more time to make a nice, artistic grid you can put up on a wall. Find grids in scientific media (they will probably have numbers or symbols) or in art and design. Ask "How many?" questions about combinations, which lead to multiplication. For example, a grid for three heads and four bodies has twelve chimeras total, because 3x4=12. Take turns posing puzzles with grid parts missing, or mixed up in wrong places.

As you read fairy tales or science news, keep an eye on combinations. Combinations of any two variables can be represented as grids. For example, luminosity and temperature defines different types of stars, such as a red dwarf or a blue giant. Any parent who sent a toddler (or sometimes a spouse) for "large spoons" or "red socks" and got wrong items back knows it's a challenge to sort silverware or clothes by a combination of two variables!

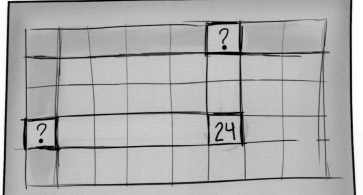

Where in the table does a particular combination go? Where is the cell where the bird-dog "lives"? Toddlers will find the task easier if the table is almost filled, with just a couple of empty cells where their piece can go. For older children, ask "Where can 24 go in the multiplication table?" Pose the opposite question: what should go into a particular cell?

Ask kids how many possible combinations you can make with a certain number of heads and bodies. Kids can use a grid to show the reasoning behind their answers. Figure out how many possible ways you can put together a cut-up grid so it still has the structure.

THE THREE BEARS AND THE MIDDLE WAY

Role play "The Three Bears" fairy tale with three toys or pictures. Find objects in three sizes (clothes, spoons, plates, chairs), and place in front of bears, in rows. Now find some other qualities of these objects – for example, softness of chairs or heat of porridge on the plates. What do you need to do to your grid so these other qualities are sorted as they are in the tale – with the baby bear's object in the middle?

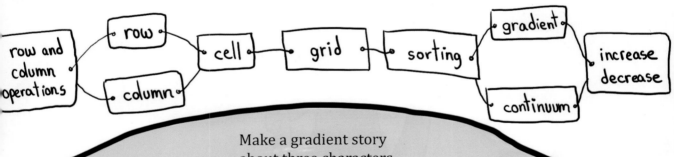

Make your own "gradient stories" with toys. Select sets of your child's favorite toys or pictures – horses, trucks, dolls – in groups of three or more sizes, and then make and find appropriately-sized objects for them. Use all senses for your gradients and invite kids to invent their own ways to sort: sound (loud to quiet, high to low), tone (dark to light), texture (rough to smooth), weight (heavy to light), and so on.

Make a gradient story about three characters, with several sets of objects sorted into a grid by their size. Use three planks or strips of paper under three columns, one per character. Now give your story different twists! What if sorting was the opposite, with the littlest character always getting the largest objects? A child may like this turn of events! You can change stories by moving whole columns in your grid. This helps children to see the structure of the grid. How many different stories can you make this way?

Explore color value and hues with gradients. Pour the same amount of water into several bowls, and add some food coloring to the first. Double the amount of food coloring for each following bowl, compared to the previous one. You can create beautiful artwork, such as collages, out of samples of paint chips, sorted into gradients by hue and value.

Help kids refine their sorting and work with more subtle variations. Investigate the different kinds of gradients professionals use in their work, as well as professional terms and measuring tools.

Make the differences more obvious. Babies can distinguish properties of objects at birth, but they are easily distracted by multiple properties of the same object. Try to find or make objects that are identical except for that one property, such as nesting dolls of the same color and shape.

Go on a scavenger hunt! You can find and make gradients about anything, from spaceships by size to xylophone notes by key. Play the game where one person closes the eyes, the other removes several pieces from a long gradient, and the first one then guesses correct places for pieces. This is a challenging game for sounds or textures, even for adults.

Use gradients to make objects and conditions fit your needs. How bright does your room need to be to study the best? Experiment with a dimmer. Do you need to wiggle more or less to concentrate? Where exactly are you, this very moment, on the wiggly gradient? Train the senses to recognize subtler distinctions in the areas your child loves, such as art gradients (hue, value), music gradients (pitch, loudness), sports (the strength of a kick), and so on.

Think of how to represent qualities of objects without using objects themselves. You can draw sizes to scale or use numbers (with older kids). There are names for colors and symbols for notes. What about textures or temperatures? Investigate the history of representations, their names and measurements, from color swatches to spectrometers.

Play blindfolded! Find the smallest of the toys by touch, in a bag, without looking inside! Many kids love to sort sandpaper by roughness or containers by weight, blindfolded.

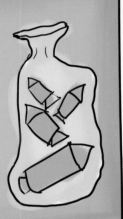

Play a stepping or jumping gradient game. Mark a starting line and invite your child to take a small step from it. Mark his new location. Now invite the child to make a larger step. Make another mark. Keep until you can't make steps any larger!

Take turns finding opposites, extremes, or antonyms. Then find the middle way between them. This is a good car game or party game for all ages. What is between night and day? Between black and white (easy)? Between green and red (use the spectrum)? Between acquitting and convicting? List your insights in a grid. You can use computer antonym finders or lists for test prep to find challenging opposites. Discuss cultural traditions such as Aristotelian "middle state" or Buddhist "middle path."

MULTIPLICATION TOWERS

Prepare several colors of blocks, and a grid. The first row will have towers made out of one, two, three and so on blocks of the same color, for example, green. The second row will have towers made of one green, one red; two green, two red; three green, three red blocks and so on. In the third row, there will be three colors in each cell. For example, the tower in the third cell of the third row will have nine blocks.

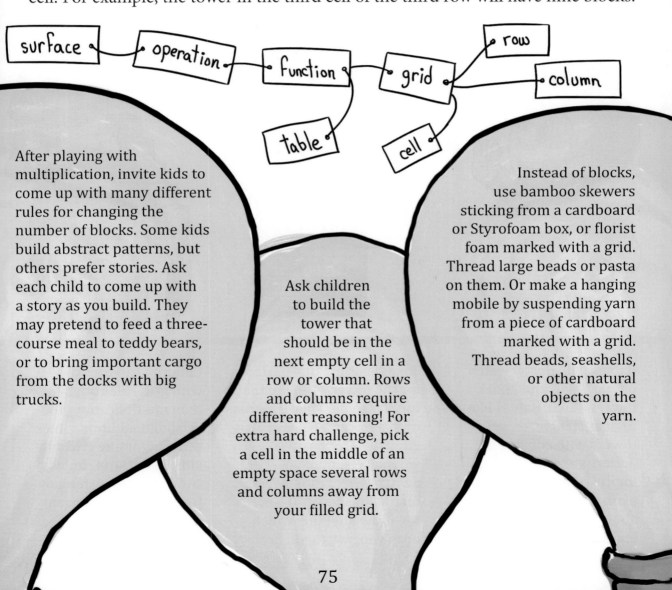

After playing with multiplication, invite kids to come up with many different rules for changing the number of blocks. Some kids build abstract patterns, but others prefer stories. Ask each child to come up with a story as you build. They may pretend to feed a three-course meal to teddy bears, or to bring important cargo from the docks with big trucks.

Ask children to build the tower that should be in the next empty cell in a row or column. Rows and columns require different reasoning! For extra hard challenge, pick a cell in the middle of an empty space several rows and columns away from your filled grid.

Instead of blocks, use bamboo skewers sticking from a cardboard or Styrofoam box, or florist foam marked with a grid. Thread large beads or pasta on them. Or make a hanging mobile by suspending yarn from a piece of cardboard marked with a grid. Thread beads, seashells, or other natural objects on the yarn.

Sometimes kids come up with rules as they build. Help them keep patterns consistent from row to row and from column to column. If they make up a new interesting rule mid-grid, start a new grid with that rule.

Babies will mostly watch parents play, and knock towers down. Babies like regular structures, so towers with consistent patterns are more interesting to them than a plain block tower. Speak about your pattern as you build, for some math vocab.

Take turns making parts for the tower, or invite the toddler to help place pieces onto a tower. They can also guess where the towers you make should go. Switch two of the towers on the finished grid, and see if the kid finds which ones you switched.

Children can experiment with grid rules other than multiplication. You can build addition tables this way, or any grid rule kids invent. You can use covariance monster games (next chapter) to invent rules.

Think of a surface that would fit the top of the towers. Which rules create curved surfaces and which non-curved planes? How about multiplication?

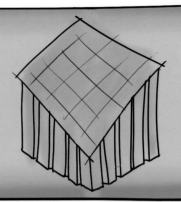

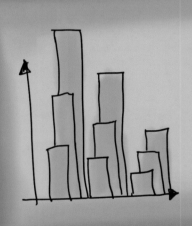

You can help older children model towers in spreadsheet software, Minecraft, or other computer platforms. Kids enjoy bridges between physical and virtual worlds, because multiple ways of building the same structure helps them to reach deeper understanding.

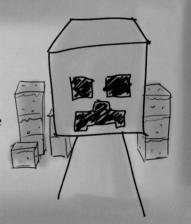

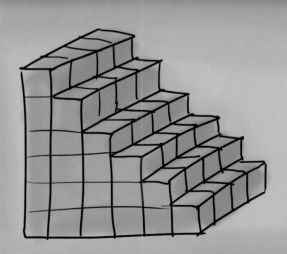

You can start with a math rule and then discover a surface it makes. Alternatively, invite kids to model objects with towers "by hand" – without rules! Can they use their tower grid to make a shape resembling a staircase, an elephant, a car, a house? This prepares kids for calculus and computer science ideas for approximating curves and surfaces.

COVARIANCE MONSTERS

Prepare a grid. Draw something simple in the upper left cell, such as a smiley face. Draw a similar face in the second cell of this row, but with a difference, for example, adding another eye. In the third cell, add yet another eye. Make predictable changes from one cell to the next. Now work by columns, changing something else, for example, adding horns.

Offer someone who has not seen your grid yet to guess how it works. Prepare an empty grid. The guesser asks what is in a cell, and you put the correct entry there. This game is similar to word-guessing games, where guessers uncover letters. Guessers uncover cells until they can deduce the whole grid.

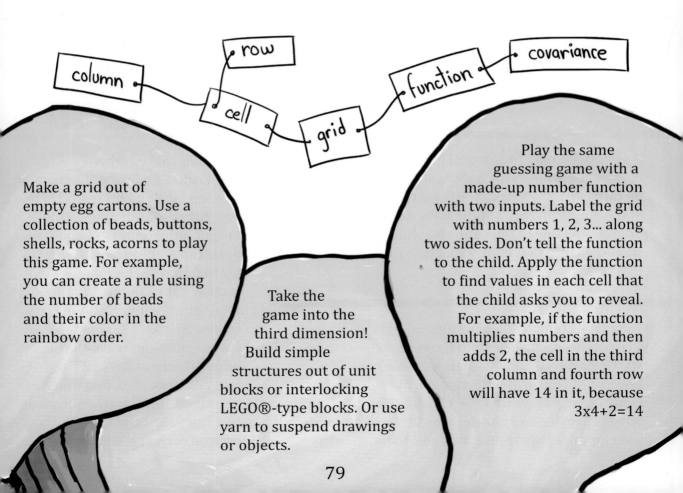

column · row · cell · grid · function · covariance

Make a grid out of empty egg cartons. Use a collection of beads, buttons, shells, rocks, acorns to play this game. For example, you can create a rule using the number of beads and their color in the rainbow order.

Take the game into the third dimension! Build simple structures out of unit blocks or interlocking LEGO®-type blocks. Or use yarn to suspend drawings or objects.

Play the same guessing game with a made-up number function with two inputs. Label the grid with numbers 1, 2, 3... along two sides. Don't tell the function to the child. Apply the function to find values in each cell that the child asks you to reveal. For example, if the function multiplies numbers and then adds 2, the cell in the third column and fourth row will have 14 in it, because $3 \times 4 + 2 = 14$

Find covariance in nature, culture, or different professions and represent it as a grid. What Montessori did with beads, you can do with growing plant measurements or company statistics.

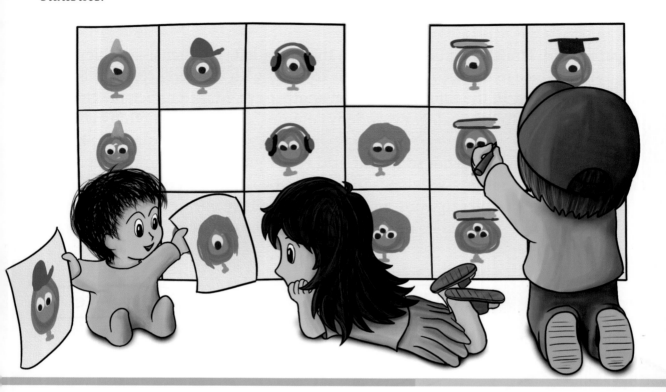

Babies don't play turn-based games. Draw covariance grids as the baby watches, and put pictures up on walls. Cut out two cells. Point at one of the empty spaces. Let the baby guess (by pointing or grabbing one of the cut-outs) which of the two should go into that empty space.

Young kids tend to change rules mid-grid, whenever a creative idea strikes. Help them be consistent by starting a new grid with their new cool rule, but keeping the old grid following the old rule. Toddlers enjoy large grids, with objects calling for different senses: heavier and heavier weights, sweeter and sweeter juice/water mixtures and so on.

Older kids make rather complicated grid rules, to make guessing harder. This leads them to explore new functions. Kids may get into arguments: the guesser may find an equivalent way to describe the same function, for example, "double the number" versus "add the number to itself." Support experimentation: try both rules and see if they always give the same answers. If so, functions are equivalent! How many equivalent ways can your child find to describe each grid's function?

Invite kids to scavenger hunts for covariance. Can you find two or more properties that change together? For example, are bigger packages more expensive per pound?

Explore music – by pitch, loudness, duration. Kids find it challenging, for example, to sing higher and higher pitches without also going louder and louder. People who are angry tend to speak louder. Asking a kid to whisper often brings peace. Where else in life do you have accidental covariance?

The more times kids play the guessing game, the more strategic they become. Strategies have to do with mathematical structures. For example, kids can ask to reveal several consecutive cells in one column, to deduce the variation along just one dimension: it is easier than covariance.

GLOSSARY

Algorithm

An algorithm is <u>a step-by-step description of actions</u>. You can conveniently reuse algorithms again and again in similar situations, and share them with others. Even very young children develop sophisticated algorithms. We usually describe them as the "going to bed routine" or the "playing house scenario". Algorithms are challenging to some people because they have many steps (assembling a bike), or because they require guessing (long division), or because they demand special skills (like manual dexterity for tying shoelaces). It often helps to capture algorithms in step-by-step pictures or symbols.

Axis of Symmetry

The axis of **symmetry** (or line of symmetry) is an imaginary line your mind's eye can learn to see in some shapes. <u>Imagine folding the symmetric shape along this line. Both sides will match exactly</u>, like two wings of a butterfly, or two clapping hands. Some shapes have no lines of symmetry within them, like one wing of most butterflies, or one hand.

Chirality

Raise your right hand in front of the mirror, wearing a glove or a mitten. Do you notice how your mirror image raises the other, left hand?! If you could reach through the mirror and give your right glove to your mirror image, it would not fit the raised, left hand. An object, such as your hand, is chiral if <u>its mirror image is different from it</u>. You can think of chirality as opposed to **symmetry**. A square, a butterfly, or any other object with line symmetry won't be chiral (but one butterfly wing is still chiral).

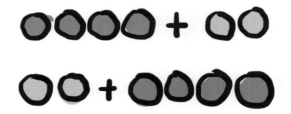

Commutative

Commuting means "moving around", and commutative means "<u>moving around without making any change</u>." For example, you can add the numbers two, five, and three in any order: the result will be ten all the same. How do you cook mashed potatoes? First, you boil them, then you mash them. Try changing the order of these **operations**. What is it you say? Mashing hard, raw potatoes does not work so well? That's because "mashing" and "boiling" are not commutative. The type of joke called "Russian reversal" plays on noncommutativity: "In Soviet Russia, TV watches you!"

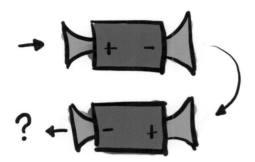

Composition of Functions

When you use the output of one **function** as the input of another, you are composing functions. Have you been on a field trip to any place that uses mass production? An assembly line for cars or computers may consists of hundreds of individual functions, all done in order. Making a bagel only consists of a dozen steps or so.

Covariance

Covariance, in this book, means that two or more things vary together. For example, bigger packages are also usually more expensive.

Cycle

Cycles are sequences of objects or series of **operations** that repeat. For example, "winter, spring, summer, autumn" is the cycle of seasons that repeats every year. There are cyclic stories and songs, like "99 bottles of beer." Many household tasks are cyclic, such as washing dishes – "lather, rinse, repeat." Cycles relate to **recursion** and **iteration**. Not all infinite sequences have cycles; for example, there are no cycles in the digits of Pi.

Domain of a Function

The domain is all allowed inputs. A coffee mug can go into a dishwasher and be expected to come out clean at the end of the cycle. An elephant or a car, on the other hand, cannot; you have to wash them by other methods. A coffee mug belongs to the dishwasher's domain, while an elephant or a car does not. In related news, you can't divide by zero (until you start working in calculus; stay tuned for our next book!) – so zero does not belong to the domain of the function that divides by inputs.

Fractal

Fractals blow our minds, because they consist of parts that are exactly the same as the whole thing, if you only zoom in. You can think of fractals as **patterns** made up of **recursions**. For example, a fern leaf consists of a stalk and leaflets. If you look closely, each leaflet consists of a stalk and sub-leaflets. And if you look even closer, each sub-leaflet... You get the picture!

Function

A function is <u>a **machine** that converts values to other values, or finds correspondences between values</u>. Function machines work by **rules** people make up. <u>The starting values are called input. The converted or corresponding values are called output.</u> The rule must find a single output for each input. Your stove is a function machine: it starts with the input of raw eggs, milk and spices, and makes the output of an omelet. The fantasy machine that starts with the same input and makes either omelets or live chickens is not a function.

Function Machine

The function machine is <u>a traditional metaphor for exploring</u> **functions**, created circa 1960s. Picture Dr. Seuss' fancy machines!

Iconic Quantity

Iconic quantities are <u>objects or actions (not symbols) that represent the quantity for you</u>. Play a quick game of associations. Finish these sentences:
- There are four...
- There are seven...
- There are twenty-four...

What came to your mind? Say, four legs of a dog, or seasons; seven days in a week, or colors of a rainbow; twenty-four hours in a day, or Chopin's preludes. There are many iconic representations for each quantity. But objects with variable or changing quantities, such as petals on a flower or pennies in jars, are not iconic.

Inverse Function

What a **function** does, <u>its inverse will undo</u>. Of course, some deeds cannot be undone. The function of "baby drops a cup of grapes on the floor" has an inverse, "parental unit crawls around, searching for grapes and putting them back into the cup". On the other hand, the function of "baby drops a cup of orange juice on the floor" and the function "you break an egg for an omelet" do not have inverses.

Isometric Transformation

Isometric means <u>the result of the transformation is the same exact size</u>. Let's say you are making stars using a cookie cutter. You are trying to make as many cookies as possible from the rolled out dough, so you turn the cutter this way and that. But no matter how you rotate the cutter, even if you turn it over completely, the size of the star and sizes of all its parts remain the same. But your transformations won't be isometric if you stretch or shrink your star after it's cut out to make the dough thinner or thicker.

Iteration

Iteration is <u>applying the same **operation** repeatedly</u>. For example, a child may break a slice of melon in half to share with her teddy bear, then break a piece of apple in half, break a piece of bread in half and so on, until all food is shared. In particular, **recursion** applies the same operation to previous results. For example, when you fold a piece of paper in half, then fold the already-folded paper in half again and so on, you use recursion.

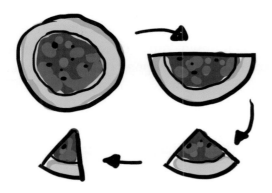

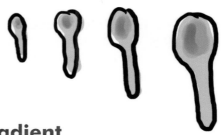

Gradient

Take all your spoons – the tiniest dessert spoon, a dinner spoon, a ladle – and lay them out from the smallest to the largest. Turn the faucet on, slowly changing it from a trickle to Niagara Falls. Think of all the books you've read, and mentally arrange them from the most to the least boring. Those are all variations of <u>ordering by a change in quantity</u>: size, volume, or the number of boredom-induced yawns. Some of the most beautiful things in life are gradients, such as the change of light at sunrise, or the change of affection as you fall in love. Unless it's love at the first sight, which is not a gradient but an instant jump in affection!

Operation

Operation is <u>another name for **function**. It is used when we focus on the **rule** of the function</u>, rather than inputs, outputs, **domain**, **range** and other aspects. In the "Stone Soup" story, new value (delicious soup) is produced from inputs of many different values (ingredients, including the stone itself). This is similar to the mathematical operation of addition, but better. A good soup, much like the eventually-cooperating village in the story, is more than the sum of its parts.

Pattern

Pattern means <u>repetition or systematic change, by **rules**</u>. You can see patterns: in arrangements of tiles on a bathroom wall; in polka dot prints on your child's rain boots; in the rhythmic flow of nursery rhymes; or in hopscotch squares on a sidewalk. As always in math, you can make up your own patterns. Fork, plate, knife... Fork, plate, knife... Fork, plate, knife... Fork, plate, knife. Now we have a table set for four, but we've also created a pattern by arranging things following the rules. As with rules and **functions**, "whatever I want to come next" won't create a pattern – the key is predictability.

Radial Symmetry

<u>Objects with radial symmetry have three or more imaginary lines that radiate from one point, called the center of symmetry.</u> The lines separate the objects into parts. Each two adjacent parts are either identical, or **reflections** of one another along the line that separates them. Starfish, tulips, daisies, snowflakes, and lace doilies all have such parts regularly arranged around centers.

Range of a Function

The range is <u>all possible outputs</u>. Once the dishwasher is done running, you can get clean dishes or, if your dishwasher isn't very good, somewhat dirty dishes. But you will not get clean, or dirty, elephants or cars out of a dishwasher. Both clean and somewhat dirty dishes belong to the dishwasher's range, while elephants or cars do not. Can you guess which **machines** have clean cars within their ranges?

Recursion

What do "This Is the House That Jack Built," slicing pizza, and stacking up blocks have in common? They are all examples of recursion: <u>applying the same **operation** to previous results</u>. This produces **patterns** that change in a self-similar ways, much like **fractals**. You put the next block on top of all past blocks; you repeat – and an amazing block tower grows till the baby knocks it down. You slice each piece of your pizza in half; you repeat – until there are enough slices for everyone. You keep on adding verses – while keeping the entire previous rhyme, much like the block tower:

This is the dog that worried the cat

That killed the rat that ate the malt

That lay in the house that Jack built.

Reflection

Reflection is <u>what a shape would see if it looked at itself in a mirror</u>. Two parts of a shape divided by the **axis of symmetry** are reflections of one another. The exact copy is not a reflection, which you can see comparing mirror images with some webcam or cellphone images. When you raise your right hand, the reflection raises its left hand while the exact copy raises its right hand.

Rotation

Rotation happens <u>when every point on an object moves along a circle, and all these circles center on the same axis or same point</u>. Every time a little girl puts on a tutu and twirls, she performs a rotation. The tips of her fingers make larger circles than her elbows, but all the parts of the girl rotate around the same axis. Going down a slide is not a rotation: elbows and fingers and all other parts move along the slide (hopefully, together).

Rule

A rule is <u>a description of how to perform actions</u>. Mathematics uses systems of objects and symbols, and rules for operating on them. Of course, we and our children encounter rules in everyday lives. Let's try making math rules! For example, the rule for + is adding quantities together. Try to invent the rule for @ and another one for #. Keep in mind that "whatever I want it to be next time" is not a rule, though kids try to use it as such!

Subitizing

Subitizing is <u>knowing how many objects are in a group without having to count or calculate</u>. Ever played a board game with dice? If so, did you have to count the number of dots on the dice, or did you recognize the number of dots without counting, just by looking? Babies can subitize to three or four, but not count, at birth. Grab a handful of beans or markers: usually, you can't subitize quantities larger than six exactly, even if you can estimate them pretty closely.

Symmetry

Symmetry means that <u>two or more parts of an object are the same or similar</u>. In physical space, symmetry leads to balance; in art, it defines order and beauty; and among people, it signifies fairness, serenity, or harmony. Slight lack of symmetry adds interest; for example, human faces normally have slightly different sides.

Tessellation

Tessellation is <u>a **pattern** of repeating shapes that can cover all space with no gaps or overlaps</u>. You can see tessellations in tiled floors, chevron rugs, soccer balls, or pineapples.

Unitizing

Unitizing is a way of thinking where <u>multiple objects or measures are considered together, as one whole thing</u>. For example, you can think of a dozen eggs as a unit – a full carton. You need to unitize to understand the modern number system. For example, to read "253" you need to see hundreds and tens as things that you can count, just as you count ones: two hundreds, five tens, and three ones. More broadly, you need to unitize to understand very large and very small objects and quantities in the universe, such as the rather puny limits of human attention (1-2 objects at once), human instant memory (5-7 objects at once), and human magnitude perception (3-4 orders of magnitude at once).